Also published by Macmillan

HE SHOOTS, HE SCORES
30 football crosswords

FOOTBALL PUZZLES
by Sandy Ransford

FOOTBALL: A fill-in book with 30 football stickers

GARY LINEKER'S FAVOURITE
FOOTBALL STORIES

'ERE WE GO!
Football Poems
chosen by David Orme

YOU'LL NEVER WALK ALONE
More Football Poems
chosen by David Orme

WE WAS ROBBED
Yet More Football Poems
chosen by David Orme

THEY THINK IT'S ALL OVER
Even More Football Poems
chosen by David Orme

FOOTBALL JOKES

Sandy Ransford

MACMILLAN CHILDREN'S BOOKS

First published 1998
by Macmillan Children's Books
a division of Macmillan Publishers Ltd
25 Eccleston Place, London SW1W 9NF
and Basingstoke

Associated companies throughout the world

ISBN 0 330 35408 6

Copyright © Sandy Ransford 1998
Illustrations copyright © Alan Rowe 1998

11 13 15 17 19 18 16 14 12 10

A CIP catalogue record for this book is available from
the British Library.

Printed by Mackays of Chatham PLC, Chatham, Kent.

Contents

For Daniel, Robert, Tommy and William

Kick-Off

Why do people play football?
For kicks.

What can light up a dull evening?
A football match.

Young Alec came off the pitch looking very dejected, and slunk into the dressing room. 'I've never played so badly before,' he sighed.

'Oh,' answered a fellow player. 'You've played before, have you?'

TEACHER: What form are you in, lad?
BILLY: Well, I scored two goals last Saturday.

DAD: How did this window get broken?
TOMMY: Er, my football took a shot at goal while I was cleaning it.

A football fan was driving the wrong way down a one-way street when he was stopped by a policeman who asked where he was going. 'To the match,' he answered. 'But I must be too late – everyone else is coming back.'

TEACHER: And why were you late for school *today*, Jimmy?
JIMMY: *I was dreaming about a football match and they went into extra time.*

A tourist visiting London stopped a man carrying a football and asked, 'How do I get to Wembley?'
   'Practise,' was the reply.

How can you stop moles digging up the football pitch?
Hide their spades.

MOTHER MONSTER: Why don't you go out and play football with your little brother?
LITTLE MONSTER: *Oh Mum, I'd much rather play with a real football.*

Why was the mummy no good at football?
He was too wrapped up in himself.

What's the best thing to do when a soccer ball is in the air?
Use your head.

What did the pitch say to the player?
'I hate it when people treat me like dirt.'

What's the difference between the Prince of Wales and a throw-in?
One's heir to the throne; the other's thrown in the air.

YOUNG FAN: Did you say you learned to play football in six easy lessons?
STAR PLAYER: Yes. It was the 600 that came afterwards that were difficult!

BRITISH PLAYER: Where were you born?
FOREIGN PLAYER: In Italy.
BRITISH PLAYER: Which part?
FOREIGN PLAYER: All of me, of course!

Which international player has the biggest head?
The one with the biggest hat.

FIRST FAN: Are you superstitious?
SECOND FAN: No.
FIRST FAN: Good. Then lend me £13 to get into the match.

What's Ryan Giggs' favourite supper?
Fish and chipping.

Which Manchester United player takes a lot of baths?
Roy Kleane.

What language would two Ruud Gullits speak?
Double Dutch.

What happened when the boy footballer married a girl footballer?
People said it was a perfect match.

When is a footballer like a grandfather clock?
When he's a striker.

When is a footballer like a baby?
When he dribbles.

When is a kick like a boat?
When it's a punt.

MATHS TEACHER: Who can explain to me what net profit is?
SMART SAMMY: When your team wins 6–0.

A football fan went to an away match and stopped for a drink at a pub on his way home. As he was leaving he saw someone had painted his car in the opposing team's colours. Very angry, he went back into the pub and demanded loudly, 'All right, then, who painted my car?'

A very large man with a broken nose and a large stick in his hand slowly got to his feet.

'I did,' he said. 'What about it?'

'Er, I just wanted you to know it's a great improvement,' stammered the fan.

When can a footballer move as fast as Concorde?
When he's inside it.

YOUNG BRYAN: Were you any good at football, Dad?
DAD: Well, I once ran down the pitch faster than any other player. And if I ever find out who put that wasp in my shorts, I'll murder him!

How do you stop a hot and sweaty footballer from smelling?
Put a peg on his nose!

What's large, grey, and carries a trunk and two pairs of football boots?
An elephant who's just joined the team.

Why did Rovers win 12–nil?
They had an elephant in goal.

What do you do if you're too hot at a football match?
Sit next to a fan.

What did the ball say to the footballer?
'I get a kick out of you.'

JIM: How should I have kicked that ball?
TIM: Under an assumed name.

HARRY: Every night I dream about football – of running down the pitch, passing the ball, avoiding tackles . . .
LARRY: Don't you ever dream about girls?
HARRY: What? And miss a chance at goal?

Why are there fouls in football?
Same reason there are ducks in cricket.

YOUNG FOOTBALLER: How do I stand for a test trial?
SELECTOR: You don't stand, you grovel.

It was a boring and disappointing match, with very little action.
    'I'm surprised the spectators don't yell at them,' said a man in the stand.
    'Difficult to shout while you're asleep,' replied his friend.

KEN: I've just been to the doctor and he said I can't play football.
BEN: Oh? When did he see you play?

MR BLACK: Why are you so sad?
MR WHITE: My wife ran off with my best friend yesterday.
MR BLACK: Oh dear.
MR WHITE: Yes, and it means we'll have no centre forward tomorrow.

Why can't horses play football?
Because they've got two left feet.

Which fish is a famous footballer?
Finny Jones.

Which footballer sails down the field like a yacht?
Gary Spinnaker.

The doctor was giving members of the team a medical. 'Breathe out three times,' he said to one of the players.
    'Are you checking my lungs?' asked the player.
    'No, I'm going to clean my spectacles,' replied the doctor.

How can a footballer stop his nose running?
Put out a foot and trip it up.

BRIAN: I love playing football. I could play like this for ever.
RYAN: Don't you ever want to get any better?

A black and white cat walked across the pitch in front of the team two weeks ago. Since then our luck has been very patchy.

How does an octopus go onto a football pitch?
Well armed!

Why was the centipede no use to the football team?
He never arrived on the pitch until half-time – it took him so long to lace up his boots.

Which animal plays football sitting cross-legged?
Yoga Bear.

What two things should a footballer never eat before breakfast?
Lunch and dinner.

Why is football like fresh milk?
It strengthens the calves.

What's black and white and wears dark glasses?
A football in disguise.

Two flies were playing football in a saucer. One said to the other, 'We'll have to do better than this – we're playing in the cup next week!'

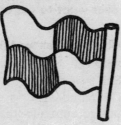

Two football fans were up in court for fighting. One fan had bitten off part of the other's ear, and the judge told him he was fined £200.

'But it was self defence,' he protested.

The judge ignored him. 'Fined £200 and bound over to keep the peace for a year,' he pronounced.

'I can't do that,' said the fan. 'I threw it in a dustbin.'

What happened when a herd of cows had a football match?
There was udder chaos.

What's the difference between a flea-ridden dog and a bored football spectator?
One's going to itch; the other's itching to go.

What can a footballer never make right?
His left foot.

POLICE SERGEANT: No trouble with football fans this week, Constable.
POLICE CONSTABLE: No, sir. Why was that?
POLICE SERGEANT: United were playing away.

How do ghost footballers keep fit?
With regular exorcise.

SPORTS JOURNALIST: Tell me more gossip about the goings-on at Rovers.
ROVERS PLAYER: I can't. I've already told you more than I heard myself.

How do you hire a professional footballer?
Stand him on a chair.

Darren and Sharon were playing football one evening, trying to kick the ball into a 'goal' marked out on a wall.
    'We'd better go, it's getting dark,' said Darren. 'And we haven't scored a single goal yet.'
    'Let's miss a few more before we go,' said Sharon.

Alan and Brian sat down to watch a video of the 1997 Cup Final. Alan bet Brian £20 that Chelsea would win. 'OK,' said Brian. 'You're on.'

Chelsea *did* win, but Alan confessed he couldn't take Brian's money, as he'd already heard the results before watching the video.

'So had I,' said Brian. 'But I didn't think Middlesbrough would lose a second time.'

What has two feet like a footballer, two eyes like a footballer and two arms like a footballer, yet isn't a footballer?
A photograph of a footballer.

Team Spirit

Which football team never meets before a match?
Queen's Park Strangers.

Which football team should you not eat in a sandwich?
Oldham.

In a theatre a magician was introducing his act. 'I will show you the mysteries of the Orient,' he said.

A voice from the audience called out, 'But what about Fulham? They could do with a bit of magic as well!'

MIKE: Did you hear that the local team now plays the National Anthem before each match?
SPIKE: Are they *that* patriotic?
MIKE: No. They play it to make sure everyone in the team can stand up.

LENNY: The Leeds manager said I'd make a great footballer if it weren't for two things.
BENNY: What were they?
LENNY: My feet.

'Our team's doing so badly that if they win a corner they do a lap of honour.'

What do you call the person in the team who carries a broom?
The sweeper.

MR GREEN: I've been invited to join the firm's football team. They want me to play for them very badly.
MR BROWN: In that case, you're just the man.

Manchester United were playing Chelsea at Stamford Bridge. A man wearing a bright red and white rosette walked up to the ticket office and asked the price of admission.

'£20, sir,' said the attendant.

'Here's £10,' replied the man. 'There's only one team worth watching.'

Jack was a keen Torquay supporter. 'All Torquay have to do to get out of the Third Division is to win eight of their next three matches,' he said.

FOOTBALLER: I've had an idea which might help the team win a few matches.
CAPTAIN: Good. When are you emigrating?

SCOTTISH TEAM CAPTAIN: How can we raise the level of our game?
SCOTTISH TEAM MANAGER: Play at the top of Ben Nevis?

What's the best US city for a football team that likes dancing to visit?
San Frandisco.

What's yellow, has 22 legs and peels off at half-time?
Banana United.

After the match the team was in the dressing room when the trainer came in and asked if anyone had seen his spectacles.

'Yes,' replied one of the players. 'They were out on the pitch.'

'Then why didn't you bring them in?' asked the trainer.

'I didn't think you'd want them after everyone had trodden on them,' replied the player.

Why did the dumbo in the team climb on to the café roof at the celebration dinner?
He'd heard the meal was on the house.

The architect was showing the team round the new stadium. 'I think you'll find it's flawless,' he said proudly.

'What do we walk on then?' asked one of the players.

FIRST PLAYER: Wasn't the captain angry when you said you were leaving the team next month?
SECOND PLAYER: Yes. He thought it was this month.

Which member of the team flies down the field?
The winger.

Which member of the team can always keep fit
providing he has a short length of rope?
The skipper.

The school football team was going to France to play
a team in their twin town.

On board the ferry, the head teacher was giving
them instructions. 'Now what would you do if a boy
falls overboard?' he asked.

'Shout "boy overboard",' called out one of the
players.

'Good,' said the head teacher. 'And what would
you do if a teacher falls overboard?'

'Er, which one, sir?' asked another player nervously.

Which football team can you find in *Whooo's Whooo*?
The Owls.

Why did the potato go to the match?
So it could root for the home team.

Why is a scrambled egg like Chesterfield in the 1997
FA Cup semi-final?
Because they're both beaten.

What happened to the snowman who left the football team?
He just drifted around.

What position did the ducks play in the soccer team?
Right and left quack.

Which football team comes out of an ice-cream van?
Aston Vanilla.

Which football team spends all its spare time at pop concerts?
Blackburn Ravers.

What was the star player awarded when he missed a penalty?
A constellation prize.

MILLY: Did you hear the football club was burgled — but all they took were the soap and towels from the players' dressing room?
WILLY: The dirty crooks!

At the annual dinner and dance of the local football club the band was so awful that when someone sounded the fire alarm everyone got up to dance.

A man was up in court charged with trying to set fire to Chelsea's grandstand. When questioned by the judge he said he had a burning interest in football.

MRS ROUND: I hear your son has a place in the school football team. What position does he play?
MRS LONG: I think he's one of the drawbacks.

A man went to meet the members of a vegetable soccer team. 'This stick of celery is our goalie; the carrots are our centre forwards; and the onions are our backs,' explained his host.

'And what's that one over there, telling everyone else what to do?' he asked, pointing to a mud-covered vegetable that was lounging around.

'Oh him?' replied the host. 'He's our coach potato.'

Why do Moscow Dynamos play such a fast game?
Because they're always rush'n'.

What team is good in an omelette?
Best Ham.

What was the monkey in the team specially good at?
Banana shots.

'Stop the ball! Stop the ball!' yelled the PE teacher to the inexperienced goalie. 'Why didn't you?'

'I thought that was what the net was for,' sniffed the poor boy.

A Sheffield man was asked why his car was painted red on one side and blue on the other. 'Because I can't decide whether to support United or Wednesday,' he explained.

FIRST PLAYER: Why do you call the team captain Camera?
SECOND PLAYER: Because he's always snapping at me.

If it takes 20 men six months to build a grandstand at the football pitch, how long would it take 40 men to build it?
No time at all, because the 20 men have already completed it!

ANDY: That new chap is a wonder player.
SANDY: Why do you call him that?
ANDY: Because I look at him and wonder if he's ever played before!

DON: How's the new player coming along?
RON: He's trying.
DON: I've heard he's very trying.

When Harry retired from the team he said he was going to work in a bank.
   'Why do you want to do that?' asked Larry.
   'I've heard there's money in it,' replied Harry.

The club advertised for a handyman, and Mr Perkins came for an interview.
   'Well, Mr Perkins,' asked the manager, 'what qualifications do you have for this job? Are you handy?'
   'I reckon so,' replied Mr Perkins. 'I only live next door.'

MANAGER: This dressing room is disgusting! It hasn't been cleaned for a month!
CLEANER: Don't blame me. I've only been here for a fortnight.

'United are such a poor team there's always a long queue at their ground – trying to get out!'

Why did the elephant paint his toenails red?
So he could hide in a pile of Manchester United shirts.

Why did the elephant wear a red and white shirt?
So he could play for Manchester United.

Weedy Willie was rather underweight and was told by his doctor that he'd be a better footballer if he put on a few pounds. 'Tell you what,' said the doctor, 'eat a plum. If you swallow it whole you'll gain a stone.'

What do you call a noisy soccer fan?
A foot-bawler.

Why did the manager have the pitch flooded?
He wanted to bring on his sub.

The leading striker kept looking at the grandstand. 'Are you thinking of kicking the ball up there?' asked another player.
    'My mother-in-law's sitting there,' explained the striker.
    'But even *you* will never hit her from here,' replied his team-mate.

What happened when the footballer went to see his doctor complaining about flat feet?
The doctor gave him a bicycle pump.

'Football, football,' sighed Mrs Jones. 'That's all you think of. I bet you don't even remember when we got married.'

'I certainly do,' said Mr Jones. 'It was the day Arsenal beat West Ham 6–0.'

'My mum says she'll leave my dad if he doesn't stop watching football.'

'Oh dear. That's awful.'

'Yes. Dad says he'll really miss her.'

PE TEACHER: Andy, you're hopeless at football, cricket and tennis. I don't think you'll ever be first at anything.

ANDY: I'm always first in the dinner queue, sir.

How many people can you fit into an empty football stadium?
Only one. After that it isn't empty any more.

GERTIE: I'm so pleased you're going to mow the lawn for Dad this afternoon.

BERTIE: Why?

GERTIE: Because then I can borrow your football.

What goes in pink and comes out blue?
A footballer who plays for a team that only has cold showers.

KELLY: While Darren was taking a shower after the match someone stole all his clothes.
NELLIE: Oh dear! What did he come home in?
KELLY: The dark!

TALENT SCOUT: Your number six looks as if he might be a good footballer if his legs weren't so short.
TEAM MANAGER: They're not that short. They do both reach the floor.

Why did the footballer put his bed in the fireplace?
He wanted to sleep like a log.

Knock, Knock on the Dressing Room Door

Knock, knock.
Who's there?
Chris Waddle.
Chris Waddle who?
Chris Waddle you do if I don't open the door?

Knock, knock.
Who's there?
Mark Hughes.
Mark Hughes who?
Mark Hughes playing for Manchester United.

Knock, knock.
Who's there?
Nigel Spink.
Nigel Spink who?
Nigel Spink when he gets out of a hot bath!

Knock, knock.
Who's there?
Aladdin.
Aladdin who?
Aladdin the street's waiting for you to come out and play football.

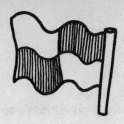

Knock, knock.
Who's there?
Accordion.
Accordion who?
Accordion to the paper United will win today.

Knock, knock.
Who's there?
Alison.
Alison who?
Alison to the football results on the radio.

Knock, knock.
Who's there?
Euripides.
Euripides who?
Euripides football shorts and you buy me a new pair!

Knock, knock.
Who's there?
Godfrey.
Godfrey who?
Godfrey tickets for the match on Saturday.

Knock, knock.
Who's there?
Juno.
Juno who?
Juno what time the kick-off is?

Knock, knock.
Who's there?
Kerry.
Kerry who?
Kerry me off the pitch, I think my leg's broken.

Knock, knock.
Who's there?
Ooze.
Ooze who?
Ooze free kick was that?

Knock, knock.
Who's there?
Al B.
Al B who?
Al B home straight after the match.

Knock, knock.
Who's there?
Felix.
Felix who?
Felixcited about going to the Cup Tie.

Knock, knock.
Who's there?
Java.
Java who?
Java spare pair of bootlaces?

Knock, knock.
Who's there?
Howell.
Howell who?
Howell you take that corner?

Knock, knock.
Who's there?
Kipper.
Kipper who?
Kipper your hands off the ball!

Knock, knock.
Who's there?
Ammonia.
Ammonia who?
Ammonia little boy and I can't run as fast as you.

Knock, knock.
Who's there?
Weed.
Weed who?
Weed like to win this game.

Knock, knock.
Who's there?
Ida.
Ida who?
Ida terrible time getting to the match – all the buses were full.

Knock, knock.
Who's there?
Howard.
Howard who?
Howard the ground is when you dive for a save!

Knock, knock.
Who's there?
Money.
Money who?
Money hurts since I twisted it on the pitch.

Knock, knock.
Who's there?
Venice.
Venice who?
Venice the next away match?

Knock, knock.
Who's there?
Francis.
Francis who?
Francis where Eric Cantona comes from.

Knock, knock.
Who's there?
Stu.
Stu who?
Stu late to score a goal now.

Knock, knock.
Who's there?
Harvey.
Harvey who?
Harvey going to have another game before lunch?

Knock, knock.
Who's there?
Waiter.
Waiter who?
Waiter minute while I tie my bootlaces.

Knock, knock.
Who's there?
Yale.
Yale who?
Yale never win if you don't play your best.

Knock, knock.
Who's there?
Luke.
Luke who?
Luke, he's just scored a goal.

Knock, knock.
Who's there?
Saul.
Saul who?
Saul over when the final whistle blows.

Knock, knock.
Who's there?
Oily.
Oily who?
Oily in the morning's the best time to train.

Knock, knock.
Who's there?
Uriah.
Uriah who?
Keep Uriah on the ball.

Knock, knock.
Who's there?
Argo.
Argo who?
Argo to Elland Road on Saturdays.

Knock, knock.
Who's there?
General Lee.
General Lee who?
General Lee I support Chelsea but today
I'm rooting for Fulham.

Knock, knock.
Who's there?
Alec.
Alec who?
Alec soccer but I don't like rugby.

Knock, knock.
Who's there?
Wooden.
Wooden who?
Wooden it be great if we won the Cup?

Knock, knock.
Who's there?
Farmer.
Farmer who?
Farmer birthday I got a new pair of football boots.

Knock, knock.
Who's there?
Nana.
Nana who?
Nana your business who we put in goal.

Knock, knock.
Who's there?
Deceit.
Deceit who?
Deceit of your shorts is all muddy.

Knock, knock.
Who's there?
Hurd.
Hurd who?
Hurd my foot so I couldn't play today.

Knock, knock.
Who's there?
Ken.
Ken who?
Ken Harry come out and play football?

Knock, knock.
Who's there?
Stepfather.
Stepfather who?
One stepfather and you'll be over the touchline.

Knock, knock.
Who's there?
Police.
Police who?
Police let me play with your new football.

Knock, knock.
Who's there?
Scold.
Scold who?
Scold wearing shorts to play football in winter.

Knock, knock.
Who's there?
Ammon.
Ammon who?
Ammon awfully good football player – can I be in your team?

Knock, knock.
Who's there?
Omar.
Omar who?
Omar goodness, what a shot!

Knock, knock.
Who's there?
Les.
Les who?
Les go out and play football.

Knock, knock.
Who's there?
Lief Eric.
Lief Eric who?
Lief Eric out of the team, he's hopeless!

Knock, knock.
Who's there?
Macho.
Macho who?
I always watch *Macho' the Day.*

Knock, knock.
Who's there?
Thermos.
Thermos who?
Thermos be a better team than this!

Knock, knock.
Who's there?
Mayonnaise.
Mayonnaise who?
Mayonnaise have seen what the ref's haven't!

Knock, knock.
Who's there?
Aardvark.
Aardvark who?
Aardvark all the way to Scotland to see
Celtic play.

Knock, knock.
Who's there?
Wanda.
Wanda who?
Wanda buy a new football?

Knock, knock.
Who's there?
Dozen.
Dozen who?
Dozen anyone in this village play football?

Knock, knock.
Who's there?
Gladys.
Gladys who?
Gladys Saturday – we can go to the match.

Knock, knock.
Who's there?
Justin.
Justin who?
Justin time to see us lose!

Knock, knock.
Who's there?
Stan.
Stan who?
Stan back, I'm going to shoot!

Knock, knock.
Who's there?
Philippa.
Philippa who?
Philippa bath tub, I'm covered in mud.

Knock, knock.
Who's there?
Willy.
Willy who?
Willy score? Bet he won't!

Knock, knock.
Who's there?
Tyrone.
Tyrone who?
Tyrone bootlaces.

Knock, knock.
Who's there?
Wayne.
Wayne who?
Wayne never stops when I play football.

Knock, knock.
Who's there?
Snow.
Snow who?
Snow use, I'm going to give you a red card.

Knock, knock.
Who's there?
Norma Lee.
Norma Lee who?
Norma Lee I play in goal but today I'm at left back.

Knock, knock.
Who's there?
N.E.
N.E. who?
N.E. body could play better than you!

Knock, knock.
Who's there?
Althea.
Althea who?
Althea later, down the club.

Knock, knock.
Who's there?
Buster.
Buster who?
Buster Old Trafford, please.

Knock, knock.
Who's there?
Ivan.
Ivan who?
Ivan new pair of boots, do you like them?

Knock, knock.
Who's there?
Anatole.
Anatole who?
Anatole me you're a hopeless player.

Knock, knock.
Who's there?
Ben.
Ben who?
Ben playing football today, have you?

Knock, knock.
Who's there?
Colin.
Colin who?
Colin and see me after the match.

Knock, knock.
Who's there?
Yolande.
Yolande who?
Yolande me some money to get into the
match and I'll pay you back next week.

Knock, knock.
Who's there?
Mister.
Mister who?
Mister bus, that's why I'm late for the match.

Knock, knock.
Who's there?
Anna.
Anna who?
Anna rack keeps you warm after football.

Knock, knock.
Who's there?
Hammond.
Hammond who?
Hammond eggs are great after football.

41

Knock, knock.
Who's there?
Gorilla.
Gorilla who?
Gorilla the sausages so we can eat before the match.

Knock, knock.
Who's there?
Harriet.
Harriet who?
Harriet all my sandwiches, now I'm too weak to play!

Half-Time

Take a quick break from the golden game to catch up on your reading. Here are some of the titles in the club library.

Embarrassing Moments on the Pitch by Lucy Lastic
Twenty-five Years in Goal by Annie Versary
Willie Win by Betty Wont
Let the Game Begin by Sally Forth
The Unhappy Fan by Mona Lott
The Poor Striker by Miss D. Goal
Why I Gave Up Football by Arthur Itis
Keep Trying Until the Final Whistle by Percy Vere
Heading the Ball by I.C. Starrs
We'll Win the Cup by R.U. Sure
Pre-Match Night Nerves by Eliza Wake
Keep Your Subs Handy by Justin Case
Training Hard by Xavier Strength
Buying Good Players by Ivor Fortune
The New Player by Izzy Anygood
Great Shot! by Major Runn
Advertising the Match by Bill Poster
Half-time Drinks by R.E. Volting

Which soccer manager is found in the greengrocer's?
Terry Vegetables.

Which famous Liverpool player was a sweeper?
Ian Brush.

DAD: Your school report is terrible. You've come
bottom out of 30 in every subject – you're even
bottom in football, and that's your favourite.
SON: It could be worse.
DAD: How?
SON: I'd be bottom out of 50 if I were in John's class,
it's bigger.

A young football fan of Southend
Wrote in rhyme – several verses he penned,
    Of their triumphs and glory,
    Their total history –
It drove all his friends round the bend.

A young football fan from Quebec
Once wrapped both his feet round his neck.
    Though he tried hard, he got
    Tied up in a knot,
And now he's an absolute wreck.

What's the best day for a footballer to eat bacon and eggs for breakfast?
Fry-day.

DAVE: Did you manage to mend my football game, Dad?
DAD: It wasn't broken — it was just that the battery was flat.
DAVE: What shape should it be?

FIRST FOOTBALLER: I received an anonymous letter today.
SECOND FOOTBALLER: Really? Who was it from?

FIRST FOOTBALLER: That dog's useless.
SECOND FOOTBALLER: How do you mean?
FIRST FOOTBALLER: I was watering the pitch yesterday and he never lifted a leg to help me.

Why did the footballer's dog run away from home?
Doggone if I know!

ERIC: My doctor says I can't play football.
DEREK: Oh, so he's seen you play, too, has he?

Why did the man become a marathon runner instead of a footballer?
The doctor told him he had athlete's foot.

A kind lady found a little boy sitting crying on the pavement. 'What's the matter, young man?' she asked.

'It's my birthday,' sobbed the lad. 'And I got a new football, and some boots, and a Manchester United shirt, and a video, and . . .'

'If you got all those lovely things, why are you crying?' asked the lady.

'I'm lost,' sniffed the boy.

MAGGIE: That football player annoys me.
AGGIE: But he's not even looking at you.
MAGGIE: That's what's annoying me!

FOOTBALLER: Two pork chops, please, and make them lean.
WAITER: Certainly, sir. Which way?

Why did the footballer call his cat Ben Hur?
It was just called Ben until it had kittens.

Why did the footballer call his dog Carpenter?
He was always doing little jobs around the house.

Two boys were walking past a house surrounded by a high wall when the owner came out holding a football. 'Is this your ball?' he demanded.

'Er, has it done any damage?' asked the first boy.

'No,' said the householder.

'Then it's ours,' said the second boy.

What position did Cinderella play in the football team?
Sweeper.

Why was Cinderella thrown out of the football team?
Because she kept running away from the ball.

Why did the thief who broke into the football club and stole all the entrance money take a shower before he left?
So he could make a clean getaway.

Did you hear about the footballer who had to lose weight? He went on a coconut and banana diet. He didn't lose any weight, but he couldn't half climb trees!

LARGE FOOTBALLER: My doctor put me on a seafood diet.
SMALL FOOTBALLER: Really?
LARGE FOOTBALLER: Yes. Whenever I see food I eat it.

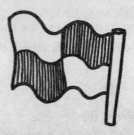

SICK FOOTBALLER: Doctor, will these little blue pills really make me a better player?
DOCTOR: I don't know, but no one I've given them to has ever come back.

DOCTOR: How's your broken rib?
FOOTBALLER: I keep getting a stitch in my side.
DOCTOR: That's good, it shows the bones are knitting.

BOSS: I thought you wanted the afternoon off to see your dentist.
MR BROWN: That's right.
BOSS: Then how come I saw you leaving the football ground with a friend?
MR BROWN: That was my dentist.

MUM: Was there a fight at the match? You've lost your front teeth.
TOMMY: No I haven't. They're in my pocket.

A house was on fire, and a fireman called up to a woman trapped on the upper floor to throw down the baby she was holding.

'I can't, you might drop him,' screamed the woman.

'I won't, I used to be a professional footballer,' yelled the fireman.

So the woman threw down the baby, and the fireman headed him over the garden wall.

Two fleas were leaving a football match when it started to rain. 'Shall we walk?' asked the first flea.

'No,' said the second, 'let's take a dog.'

How can you tell when a footballer has a glass eye?
When it comes out in conversation.

It was Christmas time, and a little boy was being asked by his teacher about the Three Wise Men. 'Who were they?' asked the teacher.

'They were footballers,' replied the little boy.

'Whatever do you mean?' asked the teacher.

'Well, the carol says "We three kings of Orient are . . ."'

Which footballer can jump higher than a house?
All of them – houses can't jump.

MRS GREEN: My husband's found a hobby he can stick to at last.
MRS WHITE: What's that?
MRS GREEN: He spends all evening glued to the football on TV.

LEN: Did you hear about the Italian footballer who belonged to a secret society that beat people up with shopping baskets?
KEN: No!
LEN: Yes. He was a member of the Raffia.

PARK-KEEPER: Why are you boys playing football in the trees?
BILLY AND WILLY: Because the sign says 'No ball games on the grass'.

FIRST FOOTBALLER: Did you enjoy your massage?
SECOND FOOTBALLER: Oh yes. I like to feel kneaded.

How did the Japanese soccer millionaire make all his money?
He had a yen for that kind of thing.

Where can a fan stop for a drink when he's driving to the match?
At a T-junction.

FOOTBALLER: I've a terrible pain in my right foot. What should I do?
PHYSIOTHERAPIST: Kick the ball with your left foot.

What was wrong with the footballer whose nose ran and feet smelt?
He was built upside down.

DAD: You must have a goal in life.
SON: OK, I'll join the local football club.

Who delivers mail to footballers?
The goal–postman.

What do you call a press photographer taking pictures of the match?
A flash guy.

Did you hear the story of the peacock who played football?
It was a beautiful tail.

What's the easiest way to find a broken bottle on the football pitch?
Play in your bare feet.

Own Goal

GARY: I'm sorry I missed the goal. I could kick myself, I really could.
BARRY: Don't bother – you'd miss.

'May I have your autograph?' a small boy asked a footballer outside the ground.

Trying to get away from him, the footballer lied, 'I really don't play football.'

'I know,' said the boy. 'But I'd like your autograph anyway.'

Sammy skived off school, saying he was going to his grandfather's funeral. Unfortunately one of his teachers recognized him at the local football match, where the score was 8–0 to the visiting side.

'So this is your grandfather's funeral?' asked the teacher.

'Looks like it,' replied the boy. 'That's him in goal.'

Young Jimmy was nervous when he first played for the team, and when they stopped for half-time he asked the captain, 'I suppose you've seen worse players.'

The captain scratched his head.

'I said, I suppose you've seen worse players,' persisted Jimmy.

'I heard you the first time,' replied the captain. 'I was just trying to remember.'

Old Butterfingers had let five goals through in the first half. 'Can you lend me 10p?' he asked the captain. 'I want to phone a friend.'

'Here's 20p,' said the captain. 'Phone all your friends.'

GOALKEEPER: Doctor, I can't sleep at night.
DOCTOR: How long has this been going on?
GOALKEEPER: About a year.
DOCTOR: You haven't slept for a year?
GOALKEEPER: I can sleep during the matches, but not at night.

It was a cold, wet, miserable day and the goalie had had a bad match, allowing several goals through. As he sat moping in the dressing room, he sniffed and muttered, 'I think I've caught a cold.'

'Thank goodness you can catch something,' said the captain.

TRAINER: You must work hard at your fitness training, Andrews. Remember, hard work never killed anyone.
ANDREWS: No, and I'm not going to be the first!

FIRST FOOTBALLER: How did you manage to break your leg?
SECOND FOOTBALLER: See those steps down to the car park?
FIRST FOOTBALLER: Yes.
SECOND FOOTBALLER: I didn't.

The team kept losing, but the captain shrugged off their run of bad luck. 'After all, what's defeat?'
    'What you're supposed to kick the ball with,' answered one of the players.

The goalie was so short-sighted he couldn't see the ball until it was too late. A doctor friend prescribed carrots to help his eyesight. The goalie ate lots of carrots, but went back to the doctor a week later, saying he still couldn't catch the ball because now every time he ran he tripped over his ears.

What gloves can a goalie see and smell but not wear?
Foxgloves.

What do you get if you cross a gorilla with a footballer?
I don't know, but when it tries to score a goal no one tries to stop it!

What's the difference between a gutter and a poor goalie?
One catches drops; the other drops catches.

What's the difference between a goalie who's asleep and one who's awake?
With some goalies it's difficult to tell!

Why is it important to a goalie that you spell words correctly?
Because if you reverse the letters in the middle of GOAL he'd spend his time in GAOL.

FOOTBALLER: You should be ashamed, giving me such a poultry salary.
MANAGER: You mean 'paltry'.
FOOTBALLER: No, I mean 'poultry' – it's chicken feed.

UP AND COMING FOOTBALLER: I've been told I have music in my feet.
VETERAN FOOTBALLER: Yes, two flats!

Did you hear about the retired footballer who bought a paper shop?
It blew away.

Why did the idiot come on the pitch dressed in diving gear?
He'd been told he might be needed as a sub.

When is a footballer in hospital with a broken leg a contradiction?
When he's an impatient patient.

Did you hear about the player who threw away his boots because he thought they were sticking out their tongues at him?

FIRST PLAYER: Why is your arm in a sling?
SECOND PLAYER: I get all the breaks.

FIRST PLAYER: I take a dim view of that captain's tactics.
SECOND PLAYER: That's because you've forgotten to take your shades off.

58

SUSIE: Why don't you like your new football coach?
SIMON: Because he told me to play in goal for the present, and he didn't give me a present!

FOOTBALLER, TO PSYCHIATRIST: I can't run, can't shoot, can't dribble, and I'm no good in goal.
PSYCHIATRIST: Why don't you give up football?
FOOTBALLER: I can't, I'm the team captain.

One player was the despair of the coach. Everything he did was wrong, until finally he got a perfect chance at goal. 'Shoot! Shoot!' yelled the coach. The player looked round in bewilderment. 'But I haven't got a gun,' he replied.

GOALIE: Where shall we put the new player?
CAPTAIN: What's his name?
GOALIE: Robin Swallow.
CAPTAIN: Put him on the wing.

CAPTAIN: Why are you late for training?
PLAYER: I sprained my ankle.
CAPTAIN: That's a lame excuse.

NICK: How old is your goalie?
MICK: Approaching 30.
NICK: From which direction?

DANNY: Did you hear about the overweight player whose doctor put him on a diet that used a lot of olive oil?
ANNIE: Did he lose weight?
DANNY: No, but his knees don't creak any more.

Why did the daft goalie take a tape measure to bed with him?
To find out how long he slept.

A weedy little man wanted to get fit enough to play football so he bought a big book on body building and worked hard on the exercises for three months. A friend asked him if it had had any effect.
    'Certainly,' he replied. 'I can now lift up the book.'

What does a goalie have when he doesn't feel well?
Gloves on his hands.

FIRST PLAYER: 'That trainer's a real angel.'
SECOND PLAYER: 'Yes, he does harp on about things, doesn't he?'

VETERAN FOOTBALLER: How old are you?
SECOND VETERAN FOOTBALLER: Thirty-two. But I don't look it, do I?
FIRST VETERAN FOOTBALLER: No, but you used to.

Two young footballers were talking about the illnesses and accidents they had had.

'Once I couldn't walk for a year,' said the first.

'When was that?' asked the other.

'When I was a baby,' replied the first.

What did the poor footballer say when the substitute changed places with him?

'What a relief!'

P.E. TEACHER: Now, Billy, you promised to practise hard at your football, didn't you?
BILLY: Yes.
P.E. TEACHER: And I promised to punish you if you didn't practise?
BILLY: Yes. But I don't mind if you break your promise.

Why was the goalie fired?
He was so gentle he wouldn't even catch a fly.

Nobody ever passed the ball to Willie, and he was moaning in the dressing room that he might as well be invisible.

'Who said that?' asked the captain.

Old Harry had been retired from the game for many years, but he still liked to tell people how good he'd once been. 'They still remember me, you know,' he said. 'Only yesterday, when I was at the players' entrance, there were lots of press photographers queuing to take my picture.'

'Really?' said a disbelieving listener.

'Yes. And if you don't believe me, ask Eric Cantona – he was standing next to me.'

It was a warm day for football and the striker kept missing his shots. At half-time he said, 'What couldn't I do with a long, cold drink.'

His captain looked at him thoughtfully. 'Kick it?' he asked.

The goalie played a dreadful match, not managing to save one ball. During the week he practised very hard for the following weekend's game. 'Notice any difference?' he asked the captain.

The captain looked at him for a few minutes before replying, 'Yes. You've shaved off your beard.'

What's higher than an Italian football captain?
His cap.

The great goalkeeper Jim 'Big Hands' O'Reilly was walking down the street. 'I recognize that man,' said Ken. 'But what's his name?'

'That's Big Hands,' replied Ben.

'Oh, really?'

'No, O'Reilly.'

Who's in goal when the ghost team plays football?
The ghoulie, of course!

Which Chelsea player is tartan coloured and chewy?
Scott Minto.

Which famous Manchester United manager was like a
Buckingham Palace guardsman who'd been run over
by a steamroller?
Flat Busby.

Which footballer ate his food very quickly?
Bruce Gobblehard.

A footballer was fond of going for long walks to help
himself keep fit. 'Every day,' he said to his friend, 'my
dog and I go for a tramp in the woods.'
   'Does the dog enjoy it too?' asked the friend.
   'Yes,' replied the footballer, 'but the tramp's getting
a bit fed up.'

Why was there a piano in the player's showers?
So they could play Handel's 'Water Music'.

CONCEITED PLAYER: I don't like this photo of me —
it doesn't do me justice.
OTHER PLAYER: It's mercy you want, not justice.

ANGRY NEIGHBOUR: Didn't you hear me banging on your wall last night?
BLEARY-EYED NEIGHBOUR: That's all right – we had a bit of a party after the match and we were making quite a lot of noise ourselves.

What belongs to a footballer but is used more by other people?
His name.

How can a footballer make more of his money?
If he folds up a note he'll find it in creases.

Why did the millionaire footballer have no bathroom in his house?
He was filthy rich.

DARREN: Did you hear about the footballer who ate little bits of metal all day?
SHARON: No.
DARREN: It was his staple diet.

Two footballers were about to retire. 'There's only one way of making money honestly,' said the first.
   'What's that?' asked the second.
   'I might have known that you wouldn't know,' retorted the first.

OLD FOOTBALL FAN: At last I've got my new hearing aid.
FRIEND: Does it work well?
OLD FAN: Half-past three.

DANIEL: Mum, can I go out and play?
MUM: What, with those holes in your socks?
DANIEL: No, with Billy next door – he's got a new football.

WAYNE: Why didn't you put a knife and fork on the table for your brother when you laid the table?
JANE: Because Mum said that when he's been playing football he eats like a horse.

Who runs out on the pitch when a player is injured and says, 'Miaow'?
The first-aid kit.

POLICEMAN: I'm sorry, but I'm going to have to lock you up for the night.
UNRULY FAN: What's the charge?
POLICEMAN: There's no charge, it's all part of the service.

Kitbag

What did the left football boot say to the right football boot?
'Between us we should have a ball.'

Why do footballers wear shorts?
Because they'd be arrested if they didn't.

Who wears the biggest boots in the English team?
The player with the biggest feet.

MUM: You've got your boots on the wrong feet.
YOUNG ALEC: But, Mum, these are the only feet I've got.

Why can't a car play football?
Because it's only got one boot.

What do jelly babies wear on their feet when they play football?
Gumboots.

TERRY: I bought one of those new paper shirts last week.
KERRY: What's it like?
TERRY: Tear-able.

HARRY: What kind of leather makes the best football boots?
LARRY: *I don't know, but banana peel makes the best slippers.*

MUM: Why are you crying?
TIMMY: Jimmy's lost his football boots.
MUM: But if he's lost *his* boots, why are *you* crying?
TIMMY: Because I was wearing them when he lost them.

What's the difference between an oak tree and a tight football boot?
One makes acorns, the other makes corns ache.

What did the boy do when his aunt sent him a football shirt for his birthday that was much too small?
He wrote her a short thank-you letter, saying he would have written more but he was all choked up.

MICKY: My brother's away training to be in a football team.

NICKY: Lucky thing! He must be quite grown up now.

MICKY: Yes. He wrote the other day saying he'd grown another foot, so my mum is knitting him an extra sock.

Dim Dennis went to a factory where football boots were made. 'What do you make them from?' he asked.

'Hide,' replied the factory manager.

'Why, who's coming?' asked the boy.

BOB: I can't find my football boots, and I've looked everywhere for them.

TEACHER: Are you sure these aren't yours? They're the only pair left.

BOB: Quite sure. Mine had snow on them.

A father asked his son what he'd like for Christmas. 'I've got my eye on that special football in the sports shop window,' replied the lad.

'The £50 one?' asked his dad.

'That's right,' replied his son.

'You'd better keep your eye on it – 'cos it's unlikely your boot will ever kick it,' said his dad firmly.

A footballer had been hit very hard on his knee, which had swollen up enormously. 'If it gets bigger I won't be able to get my shorts on,' he told the doctor.

'Don't worry, I'll write you a prescription,' said the doctor.

'What for?'

'A skirt.'

ANDY: Do you have holes in your football shorts?
BERTIE: No.
ANDY: Then how do you get them on?

What wears out football boots but has no feet?
The ground.

Why did the footballer put corn in his boots?
He had pigeon toes.

Young Chris was sent home from school for not bringing his football kit. When he returned in the afternoon he was wet through.

'Why are you all wet?' asked the P.E. teacher.

'Sir, you said I had to play football in my sports kit, so I went home to fetch it but it was all in the wash.'

When do a footballer's swimming trunks go ding dong?
When he wrings them out.

What did the football sock say to the football boot?
'Well, I'll be darned!'

FIRST SPIDER: I don't know what to get my husband for Christmas.
SECOND SPIDER: Do what I did – get him four pairs of football boots.

How short can a footballer's shorts get?
They'll always be above two feet.

SIGN ON A NEW SPORTS KIT SHOP:
Don't go elsewhere to be robbed – try us first!

Why does a professional footballer always put his right boot on first?
It would be silly to put the wrong boot on, wouldn't it?

What runs around all day and lies at night with its tongue hanging out?
A football boot.

OLDER BROTHER: Have you got your football boots on yet?
YOUNG BROTHER: Yes, all but one.

BOB: I wish I were in your boots.
ROB: Why?
BOB: Mine have holes in them.

FREDDIE: Why have you got your football socks on inside out?
TEDDIE: There are holes on the outside.

Why are a pair of much-worn football socks like a taxi driver?
They both drive you away.

GILES: What's a football made of?
MILES: Pig's hide.
GILES: Why do they hide?
MILES: No – the pig's outside.
GILES: Then bring him in. Any friend of yours is a friend of mine.

ANGRY CAPTAIN: You should have been here at 9.30.
LATE PLAYER: Why, what happened?

FIRST FOOTBALLER: Do you think it will rain for the match this afternoon?
SECOND FOOTBALLER: That depends on the weather, doesn't it?

What does a footballer part with but never give away?
His comb!

What can a footballer keep even if he does give it away?
A cold!

INSURANCE AGENT: This is a very good policy, sir. We pay up to £1000 for broken arms and legs.
DUMB FOOTBALLER: But what do you do with them all?

Why did the footballer stand on his head?
He was turning things over in his mind.

Why did the football coach have to wear sunglasses?
Because his pupils were so bright.

What's the cheapest time to phone a footballer?
When he's out!

TERRY: It's true that TV causes violence.
JERRY: Why do you say that?
TERRY: Because every time I switch on the match my mum hits me.

Why was the snowman no good playing in the big match?
He got cold feet.

Why did the bald footballer throw away his keys?
He'd lost all his locks.

How long does an Italian player cook spaghetti?
About 20 centimetres.

How does an Italian player eat spaghetti?
He puts it in his mouth.

Why did the conceited player throw a bucket of water on the pitch when he made his debut?
He wanted to make a big splash.

What does a footballer do if he splits his sides laughing?
Runs until he gets a stitch.

FIRST FOOTBALLER: When's your birthday?
SECOND FOOTBALLER: 2nd June.
FIRST FOOTBALLER: Which year?
SECOND FOOTBALLER: Every year.

A group of neighbours were organizing a village friendly match followed by a picnic and realized they'd forgotten to invite the eccentric old lady who lived on the green. So they sent a child to invite her. 'It's no use now,' said the old lady, 'I've already prayed for rain.'

MOTHER: Why are you taking the baby's bib out with you, Tommy? I thought you were going to football practice?
TOMMY: Yes, but the coach said we'd be dribbling this week.

TRAFFIC WARDEN: Why did you park your car there?
FOOTBALL FAN: Because the notice says 'Fine for parking'.

FIRST EXCITED FOOTBALL FAN: Let's take some fruit into the living room when we watch *Match of the Day*.
SECOND FOOTBALL FAN: Why?
FIRST FAN: Because I want to eat strawberries and scream!

What happens if you wrap your sandwiches in your favourite comic when you go to football practice?
You get crumby jokes!

Two boys were trespassing on the local football pitch and the groundsman came out and bellowed at them. 'Didn't you see that sign?' he yelled.

'Yes, but it said "Private" at the top so we didn't like to read any further,' replied the boys.

WAYNE: Did you hear that the police are searching the football crowd for a man with one eye called McTavish?
JANE: What's his other eye called?

A fan driving at 120 mph so he wouldn't arrive late at the match was stopped by the police. 'Oh dear,' he said, 'was I driving too fast?'

'No, sir,' said the officer. 'Flying too low.'

Two fans were discussing their packed lunches. 'What have you got?' asked the first.

'Tongue sandwiches,' he replied.

'Ugh, I couldn't eat something that had come out of an animal's mouth,' said the second.

'What have you got, then?' asked the first.

'Egg sandwiches.'

P.E. TEACHER: Now, Clarence, I'm trying to tell you how to make a tackle. I wish you'd pay a little attention.
CLARENCE: I'm paying as little as I can.

DAFT FOOTBALLER: Do you remember when I came to see you about my rheumatism and you told me to stay away from damp places?
DOCTOR: Yes.
DAFT FOOTBALLER: Well, it's much better now, so can I start having baths again?

GLEN: I had an argument with my sister. I wanted to watch football on TV and she wanted to watch a film.
BEN: What film did you see?

ANGRY NEIGHBOUR: I'll teach you to kick footballs into my greenhouse!
NAUGHTY BOY: I wish you would – I keep missing!

What happens to football fans who eat too many sweets?
They take up two seats.

Final Whistle

'Doctor, doctor, I feel like a referee.'
'So do I – let's go and buy a couple at the corner shop.'

What was the film about referees called?
The Umpire Strikes Back.

If you have a referee in football and an umpire in cricket, what do you have in bowls?
Goldfish.

What happened when the referee had a brain transplant?
The brain rejected him.

When is a trainer like a bird of prey?
When he watches you like a hawk.

What do you call a referee wearing five balaclavas on a cold day?
Anything you like, he can't hear you.

KIM: Did you say that the referee spreads happiness wherever he goes?
JIM: *No, I said* **whenever** *he goes.*

'Off!' shouted the ref, blowing his whistle.
'Off? What for?' asked the player.
'For the rest of the match,' replied the ref.

Who hangs out the washing on a football pitch?
The linesman.

Why did the referee have a sausage stuck behind his ear?
Because he'd eaten his whistle at lunch-time.

MR BLACK: Our lad's so dumb he thinks a football coach has four wheels!
MR WHITE: *Why, how many does it have?*

When is a football coach not a football coach?
When it turns into the ground.

A football coach driver went to a garage. 'Can you have a look at my bus? I think the engine's flooded,' he told the mechanic.
'Is it on the road outside?' asked the garage man.
'No, it's at the bottom of the canal,' replied the coach driver.

Why did the football coach driver drive his coach in reverse?
Because he knew the Highway Code backwards.

Which part of a football coach is the laziest?
The wheels – they're always tyred.

BEN: Our team's just bought a baby coach to carry us from match to match.
LEN: A baby coach?
BEN: Yes. It doesn't go anywhere without a rattle.

DARREN: When I grow up I want to drive a football coach.
DAD: OK, son, I won't stand in your way.

TED: Have you heard about Mrs Brown? She's left her husband and gone off with the football coach!
NED: I didn't even know she could drive!

'Doctor! Come quickly! The referee has swallowed his biro! What can we do?'
'Use another one until I get there.'

DONNY: I've never refereed a football match before. Do I have to run after the ball?
RONNIE: No, after the match.

CLAUDE: But for Herbert we'd have lost the match today.
MAUD: Is he the striker or the goalie?
CLAUDE: Neither – he's the ref.

The devil proposed a soccer match between heaven and hell. 'That wouldn't be fair,' said an imp. 'Heaven has all the footballers.'

   'I know,' replied the devil. 'But we have all the referees.'

Did you hear about the referee who got so fed up with the bad players in the teams playing that he awarded a free kick to himself?

AL: For which player did Newcastle United pay a lot of money?
VAL: I don't know.
AL: Barry Venison.
VAL: Barry Venison?
AL: Yes, they said he was deer!

Did you hear about the referee who was so short-sighted he couldn't go to sleep unless he counted elephants?

A referee was showing his friends his new stopwatch. 'It's an amazing watch,' he said. 'It only cost 50p.'

'Why is it so amazing?'

'Because every time I look at it I'm amazed it's still working.'

One day when United were playing, the referee didn't turn up, so the captain asked if there was anyone among the spectators with refereeing experience. A man stepped forward.

'Have you refereed before?' asked the captain.

'Certainly,' said the man. 'And if you don't believe me, ask my three friends here.'

'I'm sorry,' said the captain. 'But I don't think we can use you.'

'Why not?'

'You can't be a real referee because no real referee *has* three friends.'

Why is a referee like a kettle?
They both whistle when they're hot.

Which footballer keeps the house warm in winter?
Andy Coal (Cole).

Which footballer is related to Donald Duck?
Chris Waddle.

Which midfield player is found in a
hamburger?
Paul Mince (Ince).

Why was Mark Hughes forbidden to join a trade
union?
He's a well-known striker.

REFEREE: Will I be able to see right across the pitch
with these new glasses?
OPTICIAN: Yes.
REFEREE: That's wonderful! I never could with the old
ones.

Three footballers got caught out in the snow, but only
two got their hair wet. Why?
The other one was bald!

Why is a football crowd learning to sing like a person
opening a tin of sardines?
They both have trouble with the key.

BEN: I hear that new player's father is an optician.
**LEN: Is that why he keeps making such a
spectacle of himself?**

A lad going home from playing football in the park
saw a beautiful new car parked up the road from his
house. He bounced the ball on and off its bumpers,
but when he bounced it on the windscreen it
smashed in pieces. The boy's father, who was coming
to collect him, saw what happened, and shouted
angrily, 'Didn't I tell you? If you burst that football I'm
not buying you another!'

LOU: Do you like the new captain?
HUGH: I can't complain. Let's face it, I daren't!

DAD: Shall I put the kettle on?
**SON: You could, but I think you look all right in
your football kit.**

FIRST FOOTBALLER: The new player isn't up to much.
SECOND FOOTBALLER: I think we should take him at face value.
FIRST FOOTBALLER: With his face, that doesn't amount to very much!

FIRST FOOTBALLER: Girls whisper that they love me.
SECOND FOOTBALLER: Well, they'd never admit it out loud!

REFEREE: I didn't come here to be insulted!
DISGRUNTLED FAN: Where do you usually go?

FATHER: You mustn't fight — you must learn to give and take.
DENNIS: I did. I gave Danny a black eye and took his football!

FIRST FOOTBALLER: That ointment the doctor gave me to rub on my knee makes my hands smart.
SECOND FOOTBALLER: Then why don't you rub some into your head?

BILLY: That new striker's a man who's going places!
WILLY: And the sooner the better!

FIRST FOOTBALLER: My girlfriend's really clever. She has brains enough for two.
SECOND FOOTBALLER: *Then she's obviously the girl for you!*

MOTHER TO MUDDY, FOOTBALLING DAUGHTER: You're pretty dirty, Bobbie.
BOBBIE: *I'm even prettier clean.*

BILL: That coach always thinks twice before speaking.
PHIL: *Yes, so he can think up something really nasty to say!*

HARRY: Our captain is a man with polish.
LARRY: *Only on his boots!*

Ned was speaking about the opposing team's striker. 'He's out of this world!' he said.

Ted grinned wryly. 'Our team often wishes he were.'

JERRY: That goalie looks very heavy, but they say he's a light eater.
TERRY: *He is. As soon as it's light he starts eating.*

Sally and Susie were discussing a particularly good-looking soccer star. 'Do you think he's conceited?' asked Sally.

'Who else has a mirror on the bathroom ceiling so he can watch himself gargle?' replied Susie.

Why didn't the conceited star wash very often?
Because when the bathroom mirror got all steamed up he couldn't admire himself!

How can you make a tall footballer short?
Ask him to lend you all his money.

United had been playing badly and their manager hired a hall in which to hold a press conference.
Afterwards, Bill said to Gill, 'Did you notice how the manager's voice filled the hall?'

'Yes,' she replied. 'And did you notice how many people left to make room for it?'

A man realized that his new neighbour was a famous football player. 'I've seen you on the TV, on and off,' he said.

'And how do you like me?' asked the player.

'Off,' replied his neighbour.